Ink & Ashes

By: SB
Illustrations by: Fatima Seehar

Copyright©2025 SB
All Rights Reserved

Letter to the Reader

Dear Reader,

If you are holding this book in your hands, then perhaps, like me, you have loved, lost, questioned, healed, and fought battles within yourself that no one else could see.

Perhaps you've found yourself staring at the ceiling late at night, drowning in thoughts you wish you could silence. Or maybe, you've felt the weight of a love that was once everything but became nothing.

I want you to know, you are not alone.

This book is not just a collection of words; it is a reflection of emotions too deep to be spoken aloud.

It is ink and ashes, the remnants of love, heartbreak, healing, and self-discovery.

Some pages may feel like an open wound; others may feel like the first breath after drowning.

 It is raw, unfiltered, and, above all, real.

As you turn these pages, I invite you to see pieces of yourself in them.

To find comfort in the chaos, clarity in the confusion, and, most importantly, strength in the pain.

Writing these words helped me navigate through the darkest tunnels of my soul. I hope reading them does the same for you.

Whatever brought you here, I want you to leave this book knowing one thing: You are capable of healing.

You are capable of moving forward. You are capable of becoming everything you once thought was impossible.

So take your time.

Breathe between the lines.

And remember, you are not alone in this journey.

With every word,

SB.

Contents

A Pocketful Sun. 1

Throwback. 2

Notes I Never Sent. 3

Bullets. 4

Age is Just a Number. 6

Love Without a Price. 7

I'm Sorry. 8

The Rain Knows. 10

Lost in the Dark. 11

Glitter. 12

Go Ahead. 14

Disgust. 16

Medusa. 18

Inconsistency. 20

A Real Smile. 21

Life's Lessons. 23

Appreciate the Journey. 24

Face It. 25

You Are More Than Your Bad Days. 26

It's Okay to Feel Good Again 27

Persistence. 28

She Was Everything. 30

Homesick. 31

One of Those Nights. 32

Can You Hear That?	33
Where Were You?	35
Almost	36
The Truth About Numbers	37
Euphoria	38
Break	39
Something About You	40
Motion	41
Fading Connection	42
Never Thought	43
Mirage	44
Detachment	45
Space	46
Static	47
Dear Mama,	49
It's Been a While	50
Burned	51
Life Lessons	52
I Can't Believe How Alive I Felt	53
Are You Real?	54
Unspoken Truth	55
Steps	56
To the Girl Who Broke Me	57
Why?	59
The Truth About Friendship	60
The Illusion of Light	61

For the Love I Haven't Met Yet	62
Dear God.	63
Eruption.	64
Text Me First.	65
Burning.	66
A Prayer Under the Night Sky.	67
Blessings.	68
It's Okay.	69
Lies.	70
Just Peace.	71
Transformation.	72
Reflect.	73
Realization.	74
Distant.	75
Open Your Eyes.	76
Tunnel.	77
Baby Girl.	78
I Had to Stop.	79
Hallucination.	80
When Life Feels Fragile.	82
Birthday Card.	83
Conflict.	84
Darkness.	85
"What's Wrong?"	86
I Hate You.	87
The Works of My Mind.	89

Love, but Make It Tease	90
Not Without a Fight.	91
Rehab.	92
Thank You.	93
Never Thought.	95
Stranger.	97
Falling Leaves.	99
Your Story Isn't Over.	100
Fading Reflections.	101
Collapsed Stars.	102
You Are Love.	103
A New Year's Gift.	104
Maturity.	105
The Weight of a Book.	106
Loud Silence.	107
Giving.	108
Rebirth.	109
The Weight of Silence.	110
Left Behind.	111
Burnt Bridges, Scorched Pages.	112
The Art of Forgetting.	113
Rebuilding.	114
The Final Goodbye.	115
The Mirror Lies.	116
Sunlit Reverie.	117
When the Wind Speaks.	118

Echoes in an Empty Room.	119
Borrowed Time.	120
Moonlight Confessions.	121
A Table for One.	122
Time Didn't Heal.	123
I Belong to No One.	124
Mirage Of Us.	125
Was Love Ever Meant for Me?	126
The Sound of Letting Go.	127
Fragments of Silence.	128
Fleeting Echoes.	129
Echoes of You.	130
Paper Thin.	131
Unfinished Sentences.	132
Hollow Home.	133
Hands That No Longer Hold.	134
The Last Goodbye.	135
Smoke And Silence.	136
Weightless.	137
Unshaken.	138
The Recipe for Laughter.	139
Golden Hour.	140
Echoes of Us.	141
Wild and Untamed.	142
The Art of Letting Go.	143
Midnight Conversations with Myself.	144

The Softest Kind of Love.	145
The Weight of Silence.	146
Moonlit Roads.	147
The Sound of Unfinished Goodbyes.	148
Chasing Sunsets.	149
The Beauty of Beginning Again.	150
Your Future Self Is Cheering for You.	151
Coming Home.	152
On the Edge of Sadness.	153
Ghost of You.	154
The Good Moments.	155
Reasons to Stay.	156
The Art of Not Taking Life Too Seriously.	157
The Kind of Happiness That Stays.	158
Healing Looks Like This.	159
For No Reason At All.	160
Little Victories.	161
Conversations With Myself.	162
You Deserve Lightness Too.	163
The Heart of Home.	164
Joy, Inconveniently.	165
Bad Days Aren't Forever.	166
The friendship checklist.	167
Joy is Rebellious.	168
I Bet You'd Ruin My Routine.	169
Joy Found Me Anyway.	170

You're Allowed to Outgrow Things.	171
Simple Magic.	172
Before It Ended.	173
Your Life is Already a Story Worth Telling.	174
It Will Be Good Again.	175
You Are Allowed to Shine.	176
A Reminder: You're Doing Great.	177
Life Advice, From Me to You.	178
There's No Rush.	179
The Official Survival Kit.	180
Some Days You're the Poem.	181
You're Trouble, Aren't You?	182
You Don't Have to Make Sense.	183
Laugh First, Question Later.	184
The Small Wins Matter.	185
You Are the Plot Twist.	186
Self-Love, Softly.	187
The Universe Has a Sense of Humor.	188
How to Be Happy (According to Me).	189
You're Allowed to Be a Little Ridiculous.	190
Someday You'll Be Glad You Didn't Quit.	191
The Good You Cannot See.	192
Congratulations: You're Weird.	193
Today is a Good Day to Begin, Again.	194
You Make Me Forget My Standards	195
Eyes That Talk Too Much	196

Safe Love 197
When Love is Easy 198
The Love That Waits Quietly... 199
Just So You Know 200
Midnight Thoughts About Someone I Haven't Met 201
Not a Fairytale 202
Loving Life, Slowly 203
If You Ever Arrive.. 204
Soft Crush 205
Almost... 206
Call Me Dramatic 207
The Story I Now Write 208

A Pocketful Sun.

Some days, happiness doesn't come in grand gestures,
but in small, golden moments scattered through the day.

Like the warmth of the sun melting through my skin,
or the sound of a laugh I didn't know I needed.
Like the first sip of coffee on a slow morning,
or the way music wraps itself around my heart.

Happiness is a touch on my shoulder,
a soft voice calling my name,
a memory that makes me smile at nothing.
It's messy hair and oversized hoodies,
it's being at peace with where I am,
not needing to chase, just to be.

And maybe, just maybe,
happiness was never something to find,
but something to carry in my pocket,
like a tiny sun, lighting up the little things.

Throwback.

Throwback to the days when we wore our dad's necktie,
drew mustaches with permanent markers,
pretending we had the world figured out.

Throwback to falling asleep in the living room,
only to wake up in bed,
as if magic carried us through the night.

Throwback to when our biggest worry
was choosing the right toy to take to school,
racing through homework just to chase the sunset outside.

Throwback to when kisses on TV made us squirm,
when love was a mystery,
and heartbreak was just a word.

Throwback to when a Happy Meal wasn't about food,
but the prize that came with it.

Throwback to when we knew nothing of love,
or how much it could hurt.

Back then, we couldn't wait to grow up,
to taste the freedom of adulthood.

Now?
We'd give anything to go back.

Notes I Never Sent.

I've written you a thousand letters,
Each one with a different ending.
In one, we find our way back.
In another, I don't even say your name.
But in all of them,
I am still the fool who writes to someone
Who no longer reads.

Bullets.

I've spent so long writing about love,
about how I lost you,
about how you chose someone else.

But I never wrote about the moments,
the words,
the **bullets** you fired straight into my soul.

There was a time when you were **fading,**
consuming the very things you swore you hated.
You weren't yourself,
and I was **the fool** trying to hold you up.

Then you looked into my eyes
and called me by **his** name.
Over. And over. Again.
Until reality snapped back,
until you saw your mistake,
and in that moment,
your face twisted like you had seen **death itself.**

Then came the shoving.
The screaming.
The fists pounding against my chest.
For the first time,
I was afraid of you.

And I should have left then.
But I didn't.

I stayed long enough to hear you say,
"You disgust me. You make me sick. I hope you die."

And that?
That was the one time I believed you.
Not the "I love you's."
Not the promises.

Just **that.**

The world may call me a fool for loving you.
For giving you years of my life,
for worshipping you like a love worth dying for.

And honestly?
I couldn't agree more.

This is what happens when you love someone
who only saw you as a way to get over someone else.

Age is Just a Number.

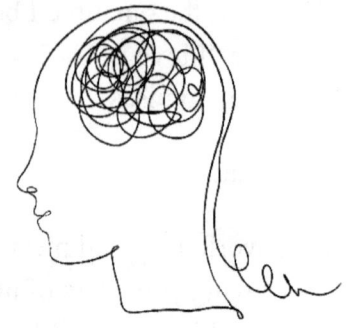

I'm not just tossing this out as a line.

I'm here to **prove** it.

I've seen people twice my **age,**

Clinging to the mind of a **child.**

Love Without a Price.

Love is not the grand gestures,
not the fireworks,
not the dramatic moments written in novels.

Love is the hand that holds yours when the night is heavy.
Love is a voice asking, "Did you eat today?"
Love is someone knowing your favorite song,
and playing it on a bad day, without asking why.

Love is sitting in silence and still feeling
understood.
Love is remembering how you take your
coffee.
Love is not needing to earn it,
not feeling like you have to be more, or less.

It just is.
And the best kind?
It doesn't come with a price.

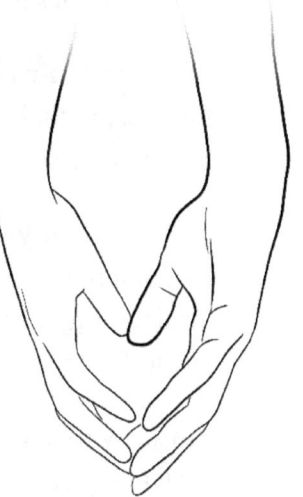

I'm Sorry.

If you're reading this,
it means you meant the world to me.
And if I could say this to you in person, I would.

But for now, let me start with,
I'm sorry.

I'm sorry for vanishing for four years,
wasting them on someone
who never deserved a second of my time.

I'm sorry to **Friends**
for missing their birthdays,
because she started fights to keep me away.

I'm sorry to **my boys**
for skipping every gathering,
for dragging them to her workshops
just to fill the empty spaces she called "friends."

I'm sorry to **my mother and sister**
for leaving early every Sunday,
for choosing her over home,
just to keep the peace that never existed.

I'm sorry to **my brother**
for turning our apartment into a battleground,
a place where he had to lock himself away
to escape her presence.

And finally,
I'm sorry to myself.

I'm sorry for wasting years
on someone manipulative and violent.

I'm sorry for pushing my family and friends away,
for letting her isolate me,
for letting her take over the space I called home
because she had none of her own.

I'm sorry for spending so much on someone
who never lifted a hand to build her own future.

I'm sorry that I broke myself for her.
That I let my love turn into chains.
That I cried over her.

That I loved her so damn much
that I'm still writing about her
when she **never** deserved a grain of my love.

I'm sorry for the panic attacks.
The anxiety.
The blackouts.
The therapy.

I'm sorry, for ever letting it get this far.

I'm sorry.
I truly am.

Yours forever, S.

The Rain Knows.

I walk under the storm,
Letting the rain do what I never could,
Wash you away.
Each drop erases a memory,
Each gust of wind silences your name.
But even when the skies clear,
The pavement still glistens,
Just like my heart,
Still holding onto what should have faded.

Lost in the Dark.

I thought I had escaped the darkness.
I thought I had reached the light.
But now, I see, **I was wrong.**

The cold creeps in,
the shadows grow longer,
and I wander, lost in my own life.

I thought I was moving forward,
but I've only been walking in circles.

The fire inside me,
the one that once kept me going,
is flickering, weakening.

And now?

I feel cold.
I feel weak.
I feel **alone.**

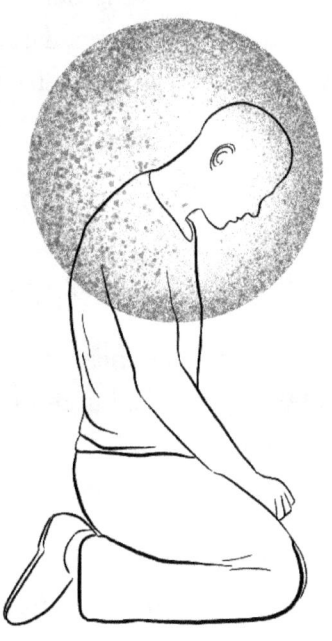

Glitter.

I dreamt of standing before a sea of faces,
my voice echoing in a darkened hall.
A crowd of strangers, a room full of friends,
and **you.**

I hid behind my hoodie, masked and nameless,
not for fear of the world,
but for fear of **scaring you away.**

I wanted them to hear me,
to feel my words, but more than anything,
I wanted **you** to listen.

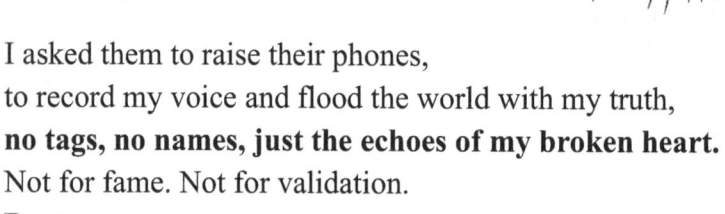

I asked them to raise their phones,
to record my voice and flood the world with my truth,
no tags, no names, just the echoes of my broken heart.
Not for fame. Not for validation.
But to prove you wrong.

I never hid you.
I never kept you in the shadows.
You were always the light I wanted the world to see.

And then I spoke,
each word a wound, each line a confession.
I fought to avoid your gaze,
but when my eyes found yours,
glittering, teary, breaking…

I couldn't go on.

The crowd roared, applause thundered,
but I stood frozen, palms damp, throat dry,
the mic slipping from my grip.

Because in that moment, I knew.
You recognized me.
And for the first time,
you truly saw me.

Go Ahead.

Go ahead, my love, **stalk my life.**
Watch me rise, one goal at a time.
Watch my smile stretch wider, my laughter grow louder,
watch me glow **without you.**

Go ahead, my treasure, **rewrite the story.**
Tell your hollow friends how I wronged you,
feed them lies you crafted with shaking hands.
Let them stalk me too,
perhaps they'll notice the cracks in your mask
before it crumbles entirely.

Go ahead, my sun, my moon, my fallen stars,
walk into the arms I warned you about,
script your love story in deception,
pose for pictures meant for my eyes.
Let your flying monkeys deliver them,
hoping to shake my soul.

I am moved.
Moved by how low you have fallen,
by the emptiness you've wrapped yourself in,
by the realization that you will **never** find
what I so freely gave.

And I, once a shattered man,
praying with tear-stained hands for your return,
questioning why my pleas were never answered,
I see it now.
God was not ignoring me.

He was protecting me from you.

I thought you were the one,
the one to grow old with,
the one to build a life with,
the one to hold my hand to the end.

What a fool I was.

What. A. Fool. I. Was.

Disgust.

I saw it. You unblocked me.
And no, my love, **don't flatter yourself.**
I didn't look because I missed you.
I didn't look because I wanted you back.
God, no.

I looked because fate needed me to see,
to confirm that the poison you fed me was real,
that the love I clung to was nothing but a fraud.

And oh, what a sight it was.
The sheer number of men you follow,
at one point, I thought I was scrolling through **his** account,
not yours.
Not my ex.
Not the girl who once whispered,
"I love you and only you."
What a joke.

The irony, the manipulation, the hollow vows,
I almost laugh at myself for believing.
For thinking that people like me still exist,
pure-hearted and honest in love.

Even when I sinned, I confessed.
I could never build love on a lie.
Especially not with the one
I once prayed to spend my life with.

But God knew better.
He knew my worth.
He knew what I truly deserved.

And it was never a girl
who finds comfort
in the attention of many.

Medusa.

The last conversation was a revelation,
a truth I never wanted but couldn't escape.
I set the trap, played the game,

watched you writhe as
your only defence

was to dredge up the past.
"I'm not here to argue about the past," I said.
And in that moment, you faltered.
No more tricks, no more venom.

Just silence.

You changed the subject,

clawing for control, asking about my book,
wondering if I'd even acknowledge
you if we crossed paths again.
I gave you a sip of your own poison.

"Would I say hi?"
"I would."

And that's what shattered you,
not the loss, not the past,
but the realization that your gaze no
longer held power over me.
Even if I saw you with him,
I wouldn't flinch.

I pity you for what you settled for,
and I pity him for what he's stepped into.

Inconsistency.

I am confused, and I know why.
A twisted game, a cycle of doubt,
one step forward, ten steps back.
I reached out, not for love,
but for closure, for clarity,
for something real in the wreckage.

"Maybe in the future," you said.
Then you erased me,
deleted my number, blocked me,
like I never existed.
And yet, you call that friendship?

I defended you when the world called you a narcissist,
but now I see,
I was your victim, and you were my mistake.

You fought to revive the past,
while I fought to let it die.
Accusations spilled from your lips,
but I was never the one who strayed.
You were. You always were.

And now, you dare to ask,
"Would you say hi if we met again?"

I would.
With a smile.
Because unlike you,
I will never need to lie to feel whole.

A Real Smile.

All my life, I placed myself beneath those I loved,
and it left me with nothing but heartbreak,
disappointment, and the sting of being used.
I never thought of **choosing me**
until the dream I had chased for five years
finally stood at my doorstep.

Stepping into that camp, I felt fear grip my chest,
the unknown stretched before me,
and for the first time, I had no idea what came next.
Six months passed in a blur,
and one morning, I woke up with a **star on my shoulder.**

It was like God had slapped me awake,
"Look at yourself. Wake the fuck up.
Appreciate what you've become."

And I saw it.

I turned a dream into reality.
Yet fear crept back in as I stood at the edge of
another unknown.
Then I heard my own voice, **louder, stronger.**

"Open your damn eyes.
You're twenty-five. You own a house,
a car, and you're working your dream
job.
Be proud.
You bled for this, you fought for this,
Now live like you've earned it."

And that's when I finally did it,
I smiled.
A real, hard-earned, battle-scarred smile.

This is me.
Welcome to my world.

Life's Lessons.

Don't grieve a love that wasn't meant to last.
Don't curse your life over those who used you.

These aren't punishments,
they're lessons.

Lessons in patience.
Lessons in recognizing the real from the fake.
Lessons in standing strong when the world walks away.

Pain is not the end.
It's the beginning of something greater.

Take every heartbreak,
every loss,
every fall,

And let them shape you
into someone stronger than yesterday.

Appreciate the Journey.

We don't always get what we want,
love,

dreams,

the perfect life.

But maybe that's the point.

Every disappointment,
every *no*,
every heartbreak,
they shape us, strengthen us,
teach us what no easy path ever could.

No matter where you are,
rising to success or starting from nothing,
appreciate it.

Because what's meant for you
will always find its way.

Face It.

Before you speak of your pain,
remember,
there are those who carry even heavier
burdens.

But that doesn't mean your struggles
don't matter.

Talking about them won't change a thing.
Standing up will.
Fighting back will.

This is **your** life.
These are **your** obstacles.

No one said it would be easy,
but nothing will stand in your way,
unless you let it.

You Are More Than Your Bad Days.

You are not the fight you had.
You are not the mistakes you made.
You are not the tear-stained pillow or the restless night.

You are the way you stood back up,
the way you kept trying,
even when you had every excuse to give up.

You are made of resilience, of soft strength,
of moments where you chose hope even
when fear felt louder.

The hard days will pass.
The heaviness will lift.
And you'll still be here,
wiser,

softer,

stronger than before.

It's Okay to Feel Good Again.

After everything you've been through,
sometimes joy feels suspicious.
Like you're waiting for the other shoe to drop.
Like you don't quite trust happiness when it shows up at your door.

But you deserve to answer it.
You deserve to open the door wide and say *yes*.
You deserve good mornings without anxiety.
You deserve peace without guilt.
You deserve smiles that don't have to be earned.

You don't have to apologize for healing.
You don't have to explain why you're
allowed to be okay.

It's okay to feel good again.
It's more than okay.
it's what you fought for.

Persistence.

I am a man who walked away
from a four-year love story
after realizing the woman I adored
was not who I thought she was.

I am a man who endured the storms,
took the blows,
swallowed the poison
because my love was **real.**

I made mistakes,
but I owned them.
Confessed, fought,
refused to lose her.

But while I was begging for redemption,
she was writing her own sins.
While I clung to loyalty,
she was rewriting the truth.

She was the woman
who once felt like my mirror,
the perfect reflection,
the effortless rhythm.

And then, she took control.

She locked me away,
isolated me from the world,
made herself my captor
while I kissed her hands in devotion.

She drained me until nothing was left,
and still, I loved her.
Still, I stayed.
Still, I believed.

Because I am in love with a narcissist.

And though she will never change,
I will.

I will set my boundaries.
I will claim my worth.
I will demand the love I deserve.

If she is truly mine,
she will **sacrifice for us.**
And if not?

Then I was never in love,
I was just another victim
who once called his captor
the love of his life.

She Was Everything.

She could brighten my mornings,
my days,

 my nights.

She was the light at the end of my tunnel,
burning so bright,
I was blinded.

Her name on my phone,
her face before me,
her laughter in the air,
each moment stole my breath.

I wanted forever.
But she didn't.

And nothing hurts more
than loving someone
who was never meant to stay.

Homesick.

I never thought I'd hear from you again…
and yet,

 I miss you more than ever.

I dream of you,
of what could have been,
of what still *could* be.

Your voice, your smile
they haunt me,
pull me back to a place I can never
return to.

You were my peace.
You were my safe place.
You were **home.**

And now, without you…
I am **homesick.**

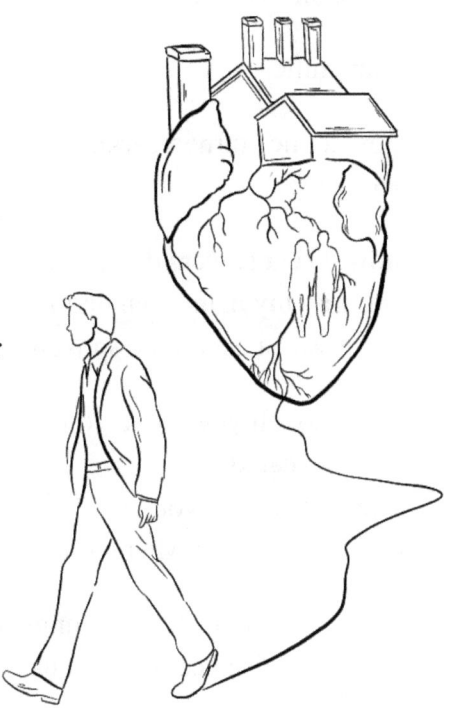

One of Those Nights.

It's one of those nights,
where my mind refuses to rest,
where all I can do is think of **you.**

Your smile,

 how it once turned darkness into light.
Your laugh,

 how it sent shivers down my spine.
The way my name sounded from your lips,
like it was meant to be spoken by you alone.

I want to tell you I love you,
but I'm scared.
Scared of losing you,
scared of a world where you're not in it.

I need you more than my lungs need air,
even with distance between us,
I feel you close,
right here,
in my heart.

Can You Hear That?

Can you hear that, baby?
That's my broken heart,

still beating.

It's all I have left,

fragile,

worn,

but yours.
Take it.

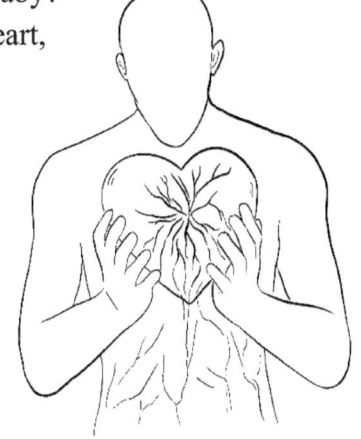

Maybe it'll be safer in your hands.

Can you hear me breathing,

 my love?
Every breath I take is for you.

You are the best thing that ever happened to me.
I don't know if it's fate or just luck,
but your presence is my peace.

The moment I see you,
a smile takes over my face,
and suddenly,

 I feel weightless,
like I'm floating,
like I'm free.

I have no better way to say it,
I need you.

You are the light at the end of my darkness.
You are home.

Where Were You?

There are nights I sit in the dark,
wondering,

where did you go?

You promised you'd always be there,
but when I needed you most,
you vanished.

Where were you when I was at my happiest,
wanting to share my joy with you?

Where were you when I needed a reason to smile,
when my world felt too heavy to carry alone?

Where were you when I stood under the cold night sky,
searching for warmth in the stars?

Where were you?

Almost.

We were almost everything,
Almost forever,
Almost the story they tell about love that never fades.
But "almost" is just another way to say
We were never meant to be.
And that is the saddest truth
I've ever had to accept.

The Truth About Numbers.

For so long,

I thought numbers mattered,
age, time, how many friends,
how long love should last.

I thought love had rules.
I thought friendship had limits.

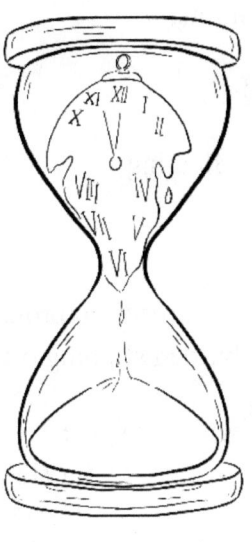

But losing someone I thought
would always be there
taught me the truth.

Numbers mean nothing.

Not years,

not miles,
not the time spent or the promises made.

Because forever isn't measured in numbers,
it's measured in **who stays.**

Euphoria.

You may not understand it now,
but when it hits,

you'll know.

It feels like floating,

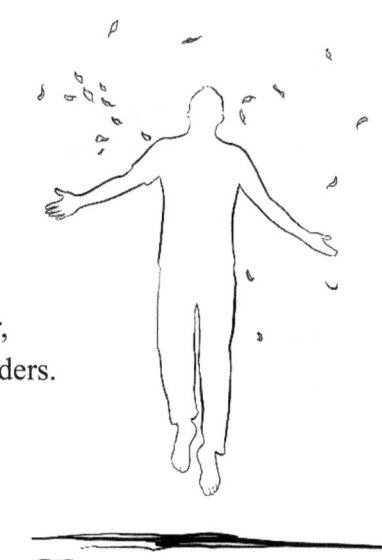

  weightless,

like the wind threading through your hair,
like every burden slipping off your shoulders.

Shivers down your spine.
Goosebumps across your skin.
Eyes closed,

  lost in the glimmer of something surreal.

You can't contain it,
your smile,

  your glow,
the way your eyes shimmer like sunlight on the ocean.

What do you call this feeling?

I call it **Euphoria.**
I call it **Freedom.**

Break.

It's been a while since I've spoken my heart,
not because I have nothing to say,
but because there's **too much.**

My mind is drowning in questions,
my heart is crushed under waves of emotions,
and my soul feels heavier than ever.

But I see it now,
the truth I tried to ignore,
the reality I refused to believe.

When I saw you that night,
disgust hit me harder than heartbreak.

You were unrecognizable.
Not the person I once loved,
not the person I thought I lost.

And suddenly, the pain that haunted me,
the questions that tormented me,
they no longer mattered.

Something About You.

There's something about you…

You make me feel at home,
yet leave me uneasy.
You make me happy,
yet keep me cautious.

I want to give you the world,
but mine is at war.
And you,
you deserve so much more.

Three simple words linger on my tongue,
but I'm too afraid to say them.

So instead,

 I'll just say this,
I'm drawn to you.

Motion.

I am healing.

Accepting every emotion,
embracing every wave that crashes over me.

There were nights I drowned in my own tears,
mornings I woke up in hospital beds,
days I spent begging God
to bring you back,

 when I thought you were my forever.

But clarity came like a storm,
washing away the illusion,
revealing the truth I was too blind to see.

You were never real.

Our love was a performance,
and you?
You played your part flawlessly.

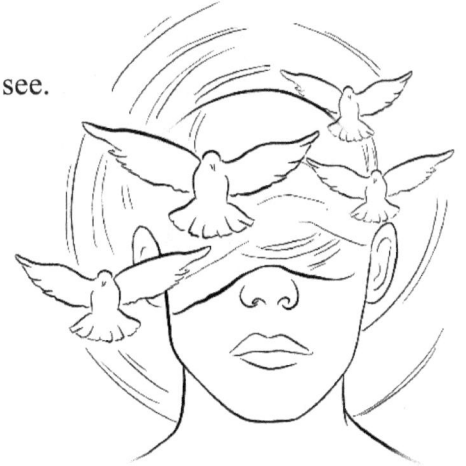

But every story has an ending.
And so did we.

And now?
I keep moving.

Not toward you.
Not toward someone new.

But toward **me**.

Fading Connection.

Last night, I almost called you.
My fingers hovered over your name,
but something held me back.

Maybe you were asleep.
Maybe you were busy.
Maybe I knew deep down,

things aren't the same anymore.

I thought about texting,
but even that felt foreign.

You used to be my safe place,
the one who made everything lighter.
Now,

 I hesitate,
unsure if I still belong in your world.

Our conversations once stretched from sunrise to midnight.
Now,

 they feel like an abandoned house,
silent,

 empty,

 filled only with the echoes of what once was.

And all that's left... is the past.

Never Thought.

I spent my life giving more than I had,
loving deeper than I loved myself.
I thought happiness came from **sacrifice**,
from making others smile,
while I stood in the shadows,

waiting my turn.

But I was wrong.

One day,

I stopped waiting.
I stopped searching for love in places it
didn't belong.
I chased dreams that were mine,

not someone else's.
And now,

I have everything I thought I'd never find,
a life I built,

a future I own.

I once believed I needed love to feel alive,
but I found something better.
I found me.

Mirage.

I still hold onto the hope
that you'll return,
even though I no longer want you.

The thought alone terrifies me,
because I know who you are now.
I know your lies, your games,
your manipulation.

And yet,

 my mind betrays me,
makes excuses for you,
defends you against myself.

I chase an illusion,
like a lost soul in the desert,
parched,

 desperate,
only to find that the oasis ahead
was never real.

One day, I will be free.
Not by running into someone else's arms,
but by finding peace in my own.

One day, I will be happy.
Not with you.
Not because of you.
But **without you.**

Detachment.

I can't keep living like this,
clinging to a false hope
you so effortlessly feed me.

You watch me from a distance,
keeping tabs, stalking my shadow,
as if that proves you still care.

But this isn't care,
this is **torture.**

Seeing your name still gives me butterflies,
but they die too soon,
buried under sorrow and overthinking.

"Why are you watching me?"
"What do you want?"

I have nothing left to give.
You wanted me broken,

  congratulations,

  you won.

I hope it makes you smile,
watching the man who once loved you
fade into nothing.

One last time,
let your smile be the thing that breaks me.

Space.

They told me to write,
but without you in my words.
Without you in my thoughts.

And my mind went blank.

I try to pour out feelings instead of memories,
but all I find is silence.
So instead,
I cry myself to sleep at night
and wear a mask by day,
smiling, laughing,
so no one suspects a thing.

I take the longest roads home,
no music,

just the noise in my head,
louder than any song could ever be.

I **hate** you
as much as you've broken me.
I **hate** you
as much as I think of you.
I **hate** you
as much as I still care,
even though you're no longer mine.

You are the **hate** of my life.

Static.

I don't know what to feel.
I don't know what to think.

The world tells me to move on,
but I stay frozen, trapped in the static,
clutching onto a false hope
that you'll come back.

But do I even want that?

After all the lies,
after all the deception,
after all the masks you wore so well,
would I really fall for the act again?

No.
I wouldn't.
I couldn't.

But I miss you.
God, I miss you.

Not a second passes
where your name isn't carved into my thoughts.
Is it just me?
Or do I haunt your mind too?
Have I ever crossed your thoughts,
or are you busy perfecting another performance,
finding another comfort,
so you never have to feel **as empty as I do?**

It's cruel,
falling this deeply for someone
who only saw me as a distraction.

I gave you my heart.
I gave you my body.
I gave you **everything** I had left of myself.
And you took it all,
shattered it,
left it in pieces
like it meant nothing.

I know one day I'll move on.
One day I'll thank myself for walking away.

But for now, I just need you to know,

You were my life.
You were my love.
You were my sun, my moon, my stars.

Dear Mama,

I'm a grown man now,
independent, standing on my own.

But tell me,

can I still run to you?

Can I hug you and forget the weight of the world,
like I did when I lost my favourite toy?

Can you hold me close,
like you did when nightmares stole my sleep?

Can you take my hand,
tell me it's okay,
like you did on my first day of school?

Just for a little while,
can I stop being an adult
and just be your child again?

Because,

 Mama,

right now,
that's all I need.

It's Been a While.

It's been a while since I let my thoughts spill.
But this time,

I won't stop writing.

I've spent too long making others happy,
solving their problems,
forgetting about myself in the process.

But what about me?

What do *I* want?
What brings *me* joy?

I search for answers, but I
find nothing.
Only silence.
Only emptiness.

I feel like I'm sinking,
drowning in a sea of thoughts,
while the world moves on without me.

No one listens.
No one sees.
No one **hears** me.

But still…
I write.

Burned.

You loved to set things on fire,
and I was your kindling.

Your fingers sparked the flame,
your words poured the gasoline.

At first, the fire felt warm,
so intoxicating, so consuming,
I forgot it was feeding on me.

Blinded by your beauty,
I didn't see the destruction in your touch.

And when you realized I was burning,
you didn't put out the flames,
you left me in them.

Watched me turn to ash,
spoke your final words,
and walked away.

Life Lessons.

Pain isn't the enemy,
it's the teacher.

Every heartbreak, every betrayal,
every moment that broke you,
they weren't meant to destroy you,
they were meant to shape you.

You'll learn that loss builds strength,
that failure fuels wisdom,
that the worst moments often lead
to the greatest growth.

So take the pain.
Take the lessons.
And let them turn you into something
unbreakable.

I Can't Believe How Alive I Felt.

I inhaled your love like smoke,
let it fill my lungs,
felt the high take over.

My heart raced,
My vision blurred.
I was floating,
higher than I'd ever been.

The rush was electric,
adrenaline pulsing through my veins,
the weight on my chest finally gone.

I felt light, so light
I could fly.

Your love burned slower than a cigarette,
but I didn't mind.

Because for the first time,
I wasn't just **existing**,
I was **alive.**

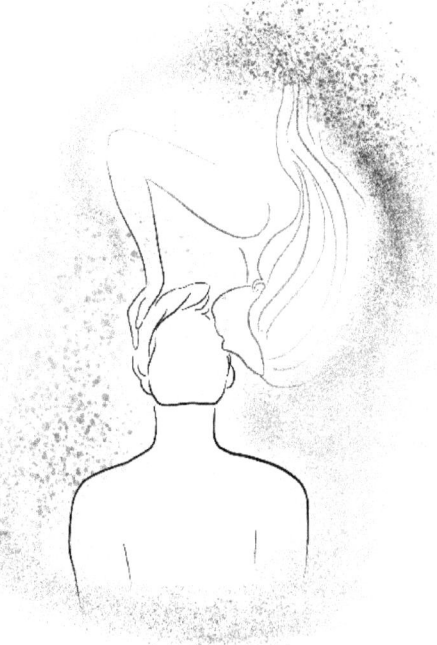

Are You Real?

It still surprises me,
you're the only one who sees through me.

You know when my smile is fake,
when my laughter is forced,
when my pain hides behind silence.

With just a touch,
you make it all disappear.

But tell me,
are you real?

Or are you just an illusion,
a figment of my mind,
a desperate hope I created
to keep myself from falling apart?

Please, tell me you're real.

Because I can't survive
another lie.

Unspoken Truth.

I once wrote about you,
but I never shared it.
I was afraid of jinxing something
that was already falling apart.

I never thought I'd hesitate
to reach for you,
but now,

even a simple text feels foreign.

You were my safe space,
the one I turned to when the world felt heavy.
Now,

 I tread lightly,
unsure if I still belong.

Our conversations once stretched from sunrise to midnight.
Now,

they feel like an abandoned house,
empty,

 silent,

 filled only with echoes
of what once was.

And all that's left is the past.

Steps.

One foot forward,

one foot back,
stuck between moving on and holding on.

I love you.
I hate you.
I wanted forever with you,
yet I wish we had never met.

You consumed me whole,
but I only ever had pieces of you.

I was trapped.
You were free.

Not even demons could inflict the pain you did,
and still,

 my heart refuses to let go.

I thought watching you watch me would move you,
but I was the only one obsessed,
searching for your name in places you no longer belonged.

Not anymore.

I refuse to keep hurting myself for you.

To the Girl Who Broke Me.

A message to the one who shattered my heart,
congratulations.
I wish you the best, and before I let you go entirely,
let me thank you for all you've taught me.

Thank you for leaving me while I was away,
for proving that **time means nothing**
when love was never real to begin with.

Thank you for the lies you whispered so
sweetly,
for showing me that **even angels can deceive**
with the softest of voices.

Thank you for your kind words,
your empty gestures,
for proving that **"actions speak louder than words"**
was nothing more than a comforting lie.

Thank you for celebrating my birthday with me,
for smiling as you blew out the candles,
only to race into **his** arms when the night was over.
You taught me that even a date of birth
could leave scars.

Thank you for throwing away three years
like they were nothing,
for teaching me what heartbreak
is supposed to feel like.

And most of all, thank you
for every second I wasted on you.
You made me realize just **how blind I was.**

Never again.

Why?

I couldn't bear the lies,
the way you said you were happy
when your eyes were drowning in sorrow.

I couldn't stand the stories of your past,
the way his name slipped so easily from your lips,
as if I was just a placeholder.

I told you the truth,
and finally, you did too.
You were still holding onto him.
Still loving him.
Still talking to him.

So I walked away.

And yet, after everything,
after all I gave,
after all I lost,

You told them **I** didn't care?
You made me the villain
when all I did was love you?

Tell me, **why?**

The Truth About Friendship.

One day, you'll realize,
the friends you thought would stay forever
are the first to walk away.

And in that moment,
you'll learn that you never needed many,
just a few who are real.

It was never about quantity.
It was always about **quality.**

Because one loyal friend
is worth more than a thousand
two-faced clowns.

The Illusion of Light.

Pain changes you.

It numbs you, isolates you,
makes you believe that feeling nothing
is better than feeling too much.

And then, just when you think you're lost,
someone appears,
your so-called *guardian angel*.

They bring light to your darkness,
give you hope, make you believe.

But then, just as suddenly,
they reveal their truth.

Your world crumbles.
The light was never real.

You wake up from the dream,
but nothing has changed.

The walls are still there.
And you're still alone.

For the Love I Haven't Met Yet

I know you're out there.
Somewhere beneath the same sky,
breathing the same air,
carrying the same hope in your chest.

I haven't found you yet
but I've built spaces in my life for you.
Left room beside me in silence,
kept stories I want to tell only once,
saved the kind of love that doesn't rush
but stays.

One day, we'll meet.
And all this waiting will make sense.

Dear God.

It's late again,
and sleep refuses to find me.

The silence is deafening,
my thoughts won't stop screaming.

As the sun disappears,
so does my peace.
And with the moon,
my sorrows rise.

I beg You,
just one night without regrets,
without memories turning into nightmares.

Let me wake up with a smile,
instead of burying my face in my pillow,
hiding from a world
that never lets me rest.

Please, God,
just let me rest

Eruption.

My mind is a volcano,
ready to erupt,
ready to spill everything I've buried inside.

Tears burn like lava,
silent screams rise like smoke.

I don't know when this will end.
Maybe it never does.

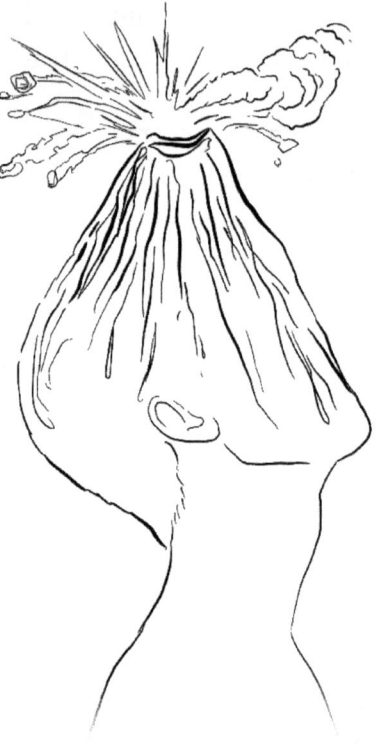

I try to speak,
but nothing comes out.
Just silence.
Just teary eyes.
Just a heart that beats too fast
for a body too tired to keep up.

No one understands.

So why keep trying?

Why keep opening wounds
for people who never cared
to stop the bleeding?

Text Me First

I won't say it out loud,
but I hope you're thinking about me right now.
Not obsessively
just enough to smile
and send a text
that sounds like
"I miss your voice"
but reads like
"hey, what are you up to?"

Burning.

Don't ask if I'm okay.
Just look into my eyes,
you'll drown in the sorrow they hold.

No smile can hide this.
No laughter can cover it.

It's heavy.
It lingers.
It burns.

And no matter how much I try to silence it,
the fire inside me refuses to die.

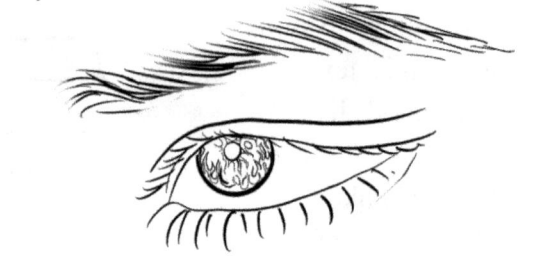

A Prayer Under the Night Sky.

Dear God,

It's late again,
and sleep won't come.

The silence is loud,
my thoughts even louder.

As the sun disappears,
my feelings sink with it,
while my mind rises with the moon.

I beg You,
just one peaceful night.

Let me sleep without regrets,
without memories turning into nightmares.

Let me wake up with a smile,
not buried beneath my pillow,
hiding from a world
that never lets me rest.

Please,

 God,
just let me rest.

Blessings.

I once thought losing you was my greatest curse.
I begged God, through tears, to bring you back.

But He was protecting me.
From the lies.
From the manipulation.
From *you*.

I spent years blaming myself,
chasing something that was never real.
But God opened my eyes,
and now, I finally see.

Your true colors burn like wildfire.
Your heart is as dark as the love I once thought was pure.

Leaving you wasn't a loss,
it was a blessing.

It's Okay.

It's okay to feel empty.
It's okay to feel lost.
It's okay to feel **everything.**

Close your eyes.
Let your heart speak.
Let the pain spill out,
free yourself from the weight you've been carrying.

Because sometimes,
you feel alone.
Sometimes,
you feel like you're falling apart.
Sometimes,
you wonder where it all went
wrong.
Sometimes,
you're just **done.**

And it's okay.

Lies.

I read something recently,

"If your ex moves on within three months,
it means the other person was there all along."

And just like that,
everything I doubted was confirmed.

No wonder my body rejected you
in the final days of us.
No wonder I couldn't meet your eyes.

You are a liar.
A manipulator.
A cheater.

I defended you,
stood by you when others warned me.
But you threw away years of love
like they meant nothing.

You blocked me,
not to protect yourself,
but to protect the tower of lies
you spent years building.

I wasn't crazy.
I wasn't paranoid.
I was poisoned by **you.**

And now, I see the truth,
you never deserved me.

Just Peace.

No reflections.
No thoughts.
Just silence.

A mind finally quiet.
A heart finally still.

No weight of the past.
No fear of the future.

Just this moment.
Just **peace.**

Transformation.

This year has been a whirlwind of **transformation** for me.

It began with **devastation** a brutal heartbreak that left me hopeless,

But **evolved** into overwhelming happiness.

I went from feeling lost to writing my first **book.**

And starting a new **chapter** on a different continent.

What started as **isolation** in misery turned into being embraced by **love,**

And **support** wherever I go.

I am forever **grateful** for every moment,

For it all **led** me here.

Reflect.

If I could change things,
would it have saved us?

Maybe we spent too much time together,
trapped in a routine that left no room to breathe.

Maybe I answered too quickly,
afraid of your accusations,
your paranoia, your control.

Maybe my only mistake
was confessing a sin
you never intended to forgive.

But the truth?
It wasn't just me.
It was **you.**

You controlled my choices,
my words, my life.
You had your backups,
while I gave up everyone for you.

I was the prisoner,
you were the warden.

And now, looking back,
I see the truth,
I didn't deserve any of this.

Realization.

I once worshipped the illusion of your return,
prayed for the chains to wrap around me again,
mistook my suffering for love.

But why would I beg for the hands that drained me dry?
Why crave the liar whose words I swallowed whole?
Why mourn the one who shattered me,
then danced in another's arms before my dust had settled?

My mind knew. My heart lied.
It painted a demon into an angel,
dragging me deeper into hell
while my soul clawed for the light.

But the moment I silenced that poisoned heart,
I **rose**.
My wings, **they grew back, stronger, wider.**
And now, I soar.

You held me down because you knew I was too much for you.
And foolish me, I begged to stay small.

But love was never your language.
You speak only in **supply**.
And for four wasted years, I let myself be yours.

Never again.

Distant.

Lately, I've been distant.
From everyone.
Even myself.

Maybe it's time
to stop making others happy
and finally think about **me.**

But what do I want?
What makes me happy?

I don't know.

I feel like I'm sinking,
drowning in thoughts I can't escape,
while the world moves on without me.

No one listens.
No one sees.
No one **hears** me.

But still…
I write.

Open Your Eyes.

I'm tired,
of this life,
of how I'm treated,
of how the world sees kindness as weakness.

People blur the lines,
between love and lust,
between loyalty and convenience,
between caring and using.

But the difference is clear.

Open your eyes.

Not all kindness is selfless.
Not all love is pure.
Not all promises are meant to be kept.

And the sooner you see that,
the sooner you'll stop letting
the wrong people in.

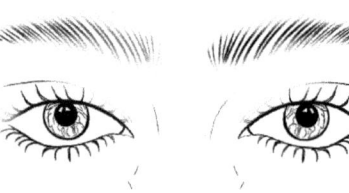

Tunnel.

She could turn darkness into dawn,
a storm into stillness, a sigh into a song.
She was the light at the end of a tunnel,
shining so bright.

Her name on my phone, **my heart stops.**
Her face in the crowd, **my breath locks.**
She was the dream I never wanted to
wake from,
the love I was ready to fight for.

But she didn't feel the same.
And the cruelest part?
Even in her distance, even in her silence,
it still broke me to see her **run from her own fears.**

Baby Girl.

You ask if I'm happy with you,
while I'm here **planning the world for you.**

Baby girl, all I need is you by my side,
because just the thought of you
makes my soul smile wide.

Let me tell you what you are to me,
and listen close to what my heart will say,

You are my princess, my
queen, my love.
Above the sky, the stars, the
moon,
beyond even Mars.

I hope you understand how
deep my love runs,
because no matter what I do,
it never feels enough.

I pray that one day, I can prove you wrong,
no matter the cost, the fight, or how long.

I Had to Stop.

It's been a while since ink met paper,
since I spilled my heart in silent confessions.

I made a promise, **no more.**
No more turning pain into poetry,
no more sleepless nights drowning in thoughts.

I once believed writing was my escape,
that spilling the words would drain the darkness,
that facing my fears on a page
would set me free.

But it started small,
one thought a week,
then every two days,
then every night.

Writing wasn't my way out.
It was the **trap** keeping me inside.

I had to stop.

Hallucination.

Have you ever woken up in the dead of night,
cold sweat clinging to your skin,
heart racing, eyes darting,
trying to remember where you are?

It happens to me **too often.**

My dreams begin soft, gentle,
flickering memories of childhood,
of laughter, of simpler days.
And then, **you appear.**

Like nothing ever changed.
Like we never fell apart.
Hand in hand, tangled limbs,
your touch still **so real.**

We inch closer, breath against breath,
lips just a heartbeat away,
and then, **the knife.**

Straight through my heart.
Your faint smile lingers
as you walk away,
again.

I wake up gasping, clutching my chest,
because the wound may be imagined,
but the pain?
The pain is real.

How is this possible?
After all this time,
I still bleed for you.

But I doubt you wake up the same.
I doubt you even remember me.

I need to stop.
Stop hurting.
Stop dreaming.
Stop hallucinating.

When Life Feels Fragile.

When someone younger than you leaves this world,
something inside you shifts.

You feel blessed to still be here,
yet shaken by the fragility of it all.

He wasn't my closest cousin,
but we were alike,
the youngest of three,
mirrors of each other.

And then,

 I saw my mother cry.
A sight I wish I could unsee.

It made me wonder,
when my time comes,
who will be left grieving me?

Birthday Card.

I wanted to be the first to say it,
Happy Birthday.

I wish your smile shines as bright as
the sun,
your beauty glows like the moon,
and your eyes shimmer like the stars.

I wish you knew,
my love for you was as vast as the
universe,
as infinite as the sky.

I saw you as something otherworldly.
I called you **Treasures**
because that's what you were to me.

I only wish you knew your worth
the way I did.

Conflict.

I don't understand you.
We are no longer together, yet you still lurk in the shadows,
watching me from a distance, breaking the very boundaries, **you set.**

Why the games?
Why the silent obsession?
If you miss me, **say it.**
Call me.
Text me.
I never blocked you, never shut the door, **unlike you.**

I know I'm blocked.
But if I were the one who kept undoing my own rules,
sneaking back just to get a glimpse,
I wouldn't just watch.
I would **speak.**

But you won't, will you?
Because this isn't about love.
It's about **control.**

You don't miss me, you miss **having me.**
You don't want me, you want me **waiting.**
You hover, you stalk, you toy with my presence,
all while **draining him dry,**
your new supply who has no idea
that your love comes with an expiration date.

Poor fool.
He mistakes your touch for devotion,
your warmth for love,
not knowing he is simply the next to **break.**

Darkness.

Night falls, but my mind refuses to rest.
Wide awake, drowning in thoughts
I wish had never been born.

"Am I good enough?"
"Am I the toxic one?"
"Why me?"

The questions **devour me.**
Maybe I'm not enough.
Maybe I was the problem.
Maybe that's why I'm alone.
Maybe that's why I'm always sinking.

I fight back forcing my eyes shut,
twisting, turning,
begging for sleep to save me.

But instead, I wake,
cold sweat, gasping, drowning,
grasping for a breath
that never quite comes.

"What's Wrong?"

Lately, every time I see a friend,
every time I sit with family,
the first thing they ask is,
"What's wrong?"

And I force a smile,
shake my head,
"Nothing, I'm fine. Why do you ask?"

They hesitate, searching my face,
then quietly say,
"You look like you're carrying the weight of the world."

And maybe…
they're right.

I Hate You.

I hate you.
I genuinely hate you.
For breaking me.
For abusing me.
For controlling, twisting, and manipulating me.

Why didn't I see it sooner?
Was I weak, or were you just **that good** at
being terrible?

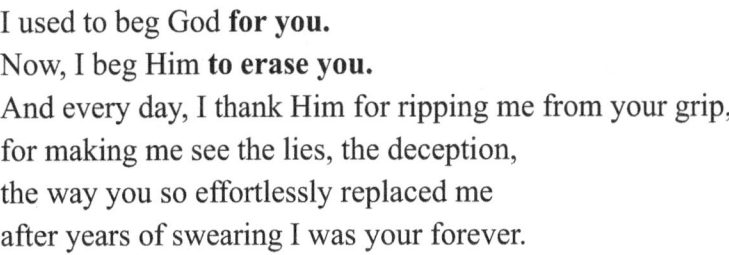

I hate that I don't hate you.
I hate that I prayed for you.
That I cried for you.
That I still think of you.
That I still see you in my dreams.

I used to beg God **for you.**
Now, I beg Him **to erase you.**
And every day, I thank Him for ripping me from your grip,
for making me see the lies, the deception,
the way you so effortlessly replaced me
after years of swearing I was your forever.

And still, stupidly, blindly,
I came back, hoping for something new.
Not to return, but to rebuild.
Not to repeat, but to move forward.

But you?
You called my presence **uncomfortable.**
Yet you still left your hooks in,
still dangled your empty words,

"We'll meet before we leave the country."
"Maybe one day, we can be friends again."

False hope.
Your favorite game.
Because you never loved me,
you just loved the way I loved you.

And I know, with every bone in my body,
no one else ever will.

The Works of My Mind.

Why do I still think of you?

What are you doing?
Are you happy?
Do you ever miss me?

My mind circles the same questions,
knowing the answers won't change a thing.
Knowing they don't matter anymore.

You discarded me.
You moved on.

And yet, no matter how busy I am,
the thought of you still slips in,
crashing through me like a storm.

"What do you want from me?"
I gave you everything,
yet you still haunt me.

You play your games,
watching from afar,
only to disappear the moment I stop looking.

But one day,
your name will no longer break me.
One day,
you'll be nothing more than a thought
that never lingers.

Love, but Make It Tease

I could fall in love with you.
But where's the fun in that?
Let's stretch it out a little
like a song you don't want to end,
like a kiss almost happening,
like a secret we're both pretending
we haven't already written in our heads.

Not Without a Fight.

I remember the nights spent by your side,
now I pray to God just to get a reply.

I'm sorry.
From the depths of my heart,
I wish for nothing but a fresh new start.

But my prayers feel like
whispers in the void,
your silence louder than
any noise.
The last thing you said
was,
"I hate you."

I hate myself too,
for the ways I failed you,
for the scars I left behind.

I know I have no place in
your life,
but **I won't walk away
without a fight.**

Rehab.

Letting go of you feels like withdrawal,
like breaking free from an addiction
that once consumed every part of me.

I was hooked on your love,
your touch, your voice,
your presence wrapped around me like a drug.

Then, all at once,
I hit rock bottom.
And I chose to go **clean.**

The freedom was intoxicating,
yet somehow, I felt hollow,
like I had carved out a piece of myself
just to survive.

God knows what you feel,
but I hope it's better than me.
I hope you can smile,
breathe,
move through the day without weight in your chest.

But I also pray for the next ones who fall for you,
the ones who will mistake your love for something real.
Because you will **never** find true love,
not when you don't understand it.

And one day, when the weight of your own lies
comes crashing down,
when your fake life turns against you,
you will regret what you did to me.

Thank You.

We have no contact now,
but there are things I need to say,
things I need to thank you for.

Thank you for the love we shared,
for the moments that felt like heaven,
for the **illusion** I once called forever.

Thank you for the memories,
the ones that still flash before my eyes
as if they happened yesterday.

Thank you for the laughter,
especially on the days when even smiling felt impossible.

Thank you for the care,
the warmth I mistook for home.

Thank you for the **trust,**
for letting me believe I was the only one
while you kept him waiting in the wings.
I pushed everyone away for you,
while you were preparing your next chapter.

Thank you for the **anxiety,**
for the panic attacks,
for making me question my sanity,
because it was you all along.

Thank you for the **time we had,**
for teaching me that time means nothing
when the love is built on lies.

Thank you for breaking me,
for bringing me to my knees,
for making me hit the ground so hard
that I finally learned how to stand.

And finally,
thank you for posting him.
For making it so clear, so easy, so undeniable.

You've shown me your worth.
And you've reminded me of mine.

Never Thought.

All my life, I placed others above me,
loved them harder than I loved myself,
cared for them while I withered,
gave them everything, only to be left with **nothing.**

Heartbreak was inevitable.
Disappointment, **a given.**

I convinced myself I was never enough,
never worthy of being chosen,
never the reason for someone's happiness.
I thought **they** deserved better,
that I was just… **not enough.**

But then, I woke up.

I stood before the mirror and finally saw **me.**
I stopped living for them,
stopped chasing approval wrapped in false smiles.

I chose myself.

And now?
I'm here.
Working my dream job.
Driving my favorite car.
Owning my own home.
Making my parents, and **myself, proud.**

I never let that feeling sink in before.
I let the weight of failed love crush me,
believing happiness could only come **through someone else.**

But I looked elsewhere.
And I **found it.**

Never thought I'd say this, but…
I'm proud of myself.

Stranger.

In such a short time,
you became someone I no longer recognize.

I tried to be a friend,
even a best friend, as you once asked.
I swallowed my pride,
stepped over my dignity,
and reached for you when I shouldn't have.

We talked for hours,
until sleep took me mid-conversation.
I woke up,
and the first name my fingers typed, **was yours.**

But you?
You made me feel like a stranger.
Like I never mattered.

You played your games again,
dodging my words,
twisting the truth,
dragging me back into **misery** like a cycle on repeat.

How foolish I was,
to think I could bring you back into my life,
to think we could be anything but a **lesson learned.**

But I saw it.
The cracks in your act.
The fleeting moments where you slipped,
where you showed **you missed me too.**

And just as quickly,
you snapped back into character.

But I'm no fool, **not anymore.**

I won't play along.
I won't fall for the illusion.
I ended it, **before you could break me again.**

Falling Leaves.

As I watch the **leaves** gently fall from the trees,

Holding on for so long before finally letting go,

I can't help but feel a few things deeply.

First,

I've come to understand that everything in life is **temporary.**

Second,

I've realized that it's okay to let **go,**

To release what we've been holding onto.

And finally,

Life,

In all it's beauty and change,

will continue on.

Your Story Isn't Over.

Maybe today feels small,
or heavy,

or stuck.
Maybe you're wondering if it's all just going to stay the same.

But listen closely,
no story stays still forever.
Even now, even when you can't see it,
life is shifting around you.

You are not trapped in a single chapter.
You are still unfolding.
Still learning, still becoming.

There are pages ahead filled with things you can't imagine yet.
new laughter, new courage, new beginnings.

Don't close the book just because today is hard.
The best parts might still be waiting for you.

Fading Reflections.

I gave them,

The **sun,**

The stars,

And the **moon…**

Every ounce of my **light,**

My warmth,

My love.

But some **hearts** are too small to hold something so **vast,**

And some **souls** never deserved the **universe,**

You were **willing** to give.

Collapsed Stars.

I used to see the universe in your eyes,
Now all I see is the black hole you left behind.
Love is supposed to create,
But all ours did was destroy.
We were once burning stars,
Illuminating the night sky,
But we burned too fast,
And now there's nothing but dust.

You Are Love.

I wanted to hold your hands,
kiss them gently between each pause,
lose myself in your eyes as I asked,
"What is love to you?"

I'd listen, hanging onto every word,
until you turned the question to me.
And I would say…

Love is your soft hands in mine.
Love is the light in your eyes.
Love is the warmth I feel when I'm near you.
Love is your laugh, your voice, your name.

Love is you in every hairstyle you've worn,
every shade of nail polish that graced your fingers.

But love is not just happiness.
Love is sadness, love is anger, love is jealousy.
Love is the ache of missing you,
the fire of knowing I can't do a damn thing about it.

Love is perfection,
but love is also torment.
Love is heaven. Love is hell.

Love… is you.

A New Year's Gift.

A new year unfolds,
carrying laughter, lessons, and loss.
But this time,
I step forward with the **wisdom**
the past year gifted me.

Maturity.

Maturity isn't measured in **years,**
but in grace under struggle,
humility in mistakes,
and the courage to choose **growth**
over comfort.

The Weight of a Book.

I poured myself into **pages,**
relived the highs and the **heartbreaks,**
stitched myself back together,
one word at a time.
Now, I wait,
will they see me in the ink?
Will they understand?
I don't know.
But I do know this:
I did it.
I am an **author.**

Loud Silence.

My mouth is **quiet,**

But my mind is loud.

My laughter is unmistakable,

And my eyes hold **warmth.**

I turn the noise in my head into thoughts,

I laugh freely with the ones I **cherish,**

And I notice the smallest details in the people,

I love.

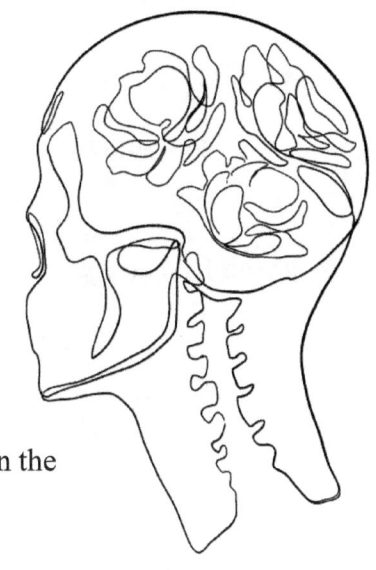

Giving.

I've **given** too much of myself to people,

Who never deserved it.

No wonder I miss who I used to be,

There's no point in **mourning** the past,

But it's a **lesson** I'll carry with me forever.

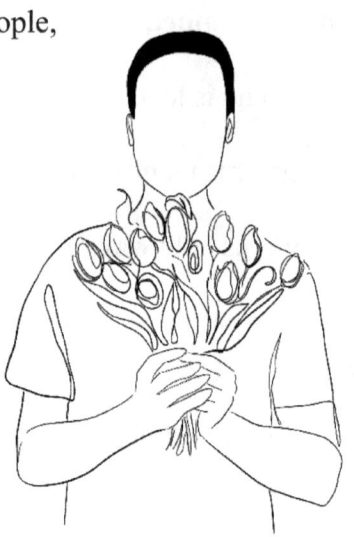

Rebirth.

I thought my life was **over** without you,

But it turned out that it was just getting **started.**

Rest in peace the person I was,

Long live the person I am.

The Weight of Silence.

Loud voices never hurt me,
It's the quiet that kills.
The space between words,
The unspoken goodbyes,
The way your name feels foreign in my mouth.
I scream inside my mind,
Yet outside, I say nothing.
The weight of silence,
Crushing, suffocating, endless.

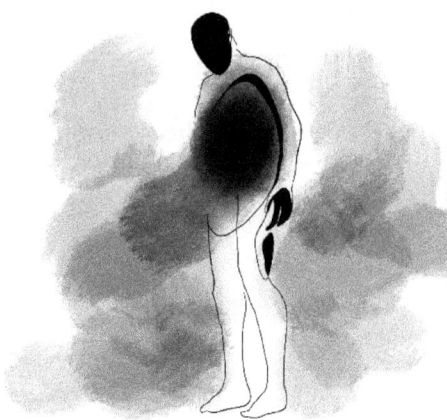

Left Behind.

I wasn't the one who walked away,
Yet I am the one who lingers.
Like an echo in an empty hall,
A song stuck in the mind of someone who no longer sings.
You moved on like I was just another passing thought.
But me?
I am still here,
Writing letters I'll never send,
Holding onto the past like it owes me something.

Burnt Bridges, Scorched Pages.

I set fire to the bridge between us,
Watched the flames dance,
Felt the warmth of destruction.
I thought it would free me,
But as the embers turned to ash,
I realized,
I still stood on the same side,
Waiting for a way back.

The Art of Forgetting.

They say time heals,
But they never tell you it's a slow death.
A fading photograph,
A scent that disappears from your pillow,

A memory that warps with time.
Forgetting isn't a moment,
It's an art,
And I am still learning how to paint my world without you in it.

Rebuilding.

Letting go isn't failure.
It's courage.
Break free from the empty promises,
shape yourself not by their mold,
but by the strength
that survived them.

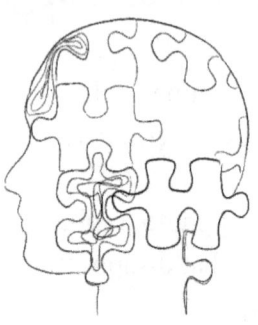

The Final Goodbye.

I imagined our ending differently,
Maybe one last look,
Maybe a final apology.
But life is cruel,
It gives no warnings,
No closure,
Just an empty space where love once lived.
This is my final goodbye,
Not to you,
But to the version of myself who once thought you were forever.

The Mirror Lies.

I look at my reflection,
But I don't recognize the person staring back.
Once, I was light.
Once, I was fire.
Now, I am just remnants of a storm,
A quiet hurricane in human form,
Waiting to disappear into nothingness.

Sunlit Reverie.

The warmth of the sun kisses my skin,
And for the first time in a while, I let it.
I close my eyes,
Feeling the breeze wrap around me like a whisper of freedom.
No weight, no past, no ghosts,
Just this moment,
Just this light,
Just me.

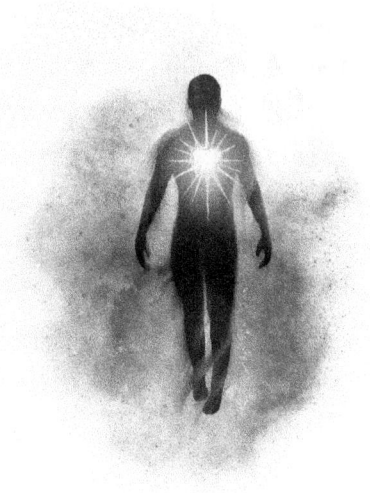

When the Wind Speaks.

Sometimes, the wind carries whispers,
Echoes of laughter,
Traces of voices long gone.
I stand still,
Listening to what it has to say.
Maybe it's just the wind…
Or maybe it's the universe telling me
That nothing truly disappears.

Echoes in an Empty Room.

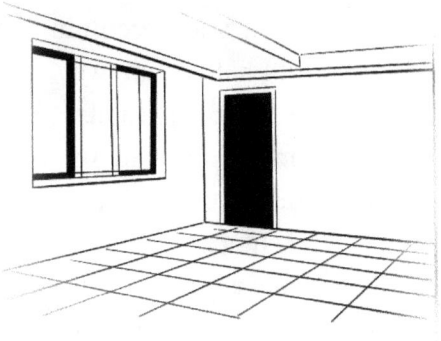

The walls still know your voice,
Even if I don't say your name anymore.
The silence should be comforting,
But it only makes your absence louder.
I could fill the space with music,
With laughter, with voices, with noise.
But I don't.
I let the echoes speak.

Borrowed Time.

I knew you weren't mine to keep,
But I held on anyway.
Like gripping sand,
Slipping through my fingers,
The tighter I held,
The quicker you left.
You were never mine,
Just borrowed time I never wanted to return.

Moonlight Confessions.

The moon has heard every word
I was too afraid to say out loud.
It knows my heartbreak,
My longings,
My silent prayers for something that was
never meant to be.
Yet, it still shines,
Unmoved, unshaken,
Reminding me that some things exist,
Even when they aren't returned.

A Table for One.

Once, I saved a seat for you.
Now, I sit alone,
Tracing the rim of my glass,
Sipping silence.
Love left,
But solitude stayed,
And I've learned to raise a toast
To my own company.

Time Didn't Heal.

They said time would heal,
That one day, I'd wake up
And your name wouldn't feel like an open wound.
But time didn't heal,
It just taught me how to live with the scar.

I Belong to No One.

Once, I lived for you,
Breathed for you,
Bent for you.
Now, I stand alone,
Unclaimed, untethered,
Belonging to no one but myself.
And for the first time,
That is enough.

Mirage Of Us.

I swear I saw you today,
Not in flesh, but in memory,
A trick of light,
A mirage that taunts my heart.

For a second, you were there,
Standing at the place we used to meet,
Your silhouette outlined by the sun,
Your laughter woven into the breeze.

I reached for you,
But you faded.
Just like before.
Just like always.

Was Love Ever Meant for Me?

I spent my life searching for love,
believing it would make me whole,
believing it would finally bring me peace.

But now?
I no longer crave it.

Was it the fear of being hurt again?
Was it the weight of lost hope?
Or was it something deeper,
a flaw within me,
something that keeps love at a distance?

I don't have the answers.

But somehow,
I can't shake the feeling
that love was never meant for me.

The Sound of Letting Go.

It doesn't happen all at once.
It's not a door slamming shut,
Not a final word spoken.
It's quieter,
Like a song fading out,
Like a whisper carried by the wind.
One day, you wake up
And realize the silence doesn't hurt anymore.

Fragments of Silence.

There are words that die on my tongue,
thoughts that drown before they reach the shore.
I have rehearsed confessions in my mind,
but silence always speaks before I do.

Between us, the space is heavy,
thick with echoes of everything we never said.
I could reach out,
but what good is a bridge if the other side is empty?

Maybe silence is its own language,
a slow-burning truth we refuse to speak.
And maybe, just maybe,
some things are meant to be left unsaid.

Fleeting Echoes.

I walked through the empty streets, my footsteps echoing in the silence of the night. The world felt lighter, yet the weight inside me remained. I wasn't carrying you anymore, but the ghost of what we were still lingered.

I glanced at the spaces we once filled, the memories still playing like old film reels, grainy and distant. The laughter, the whispers, the warmth, it all felt so close, yet so untouchable.

I don't miss you. Not the way I used to.
I miss the feeling of being wanted, the illusion of being enough.
But illusions fade, and so did you.

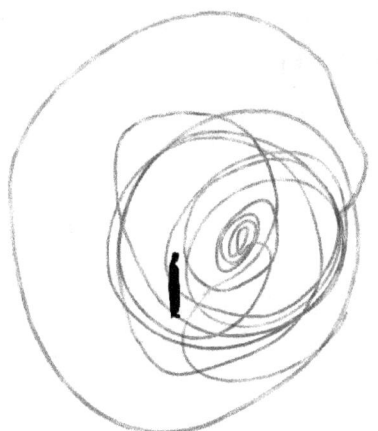

I close my eyes, inhale the cold air, and let the echoes of the past drift away.

Tonight, I walk forward.

Echoes of You.

I walk through empty streets,
Yet your laughter lingers in the air.
Every song, every whisper of the wind,
Carries a trace of you,
A ghost I can never embrace,
Yet one I cannot let go of.

I close my eyes,
And I hear you calling my name,
Not in sorrow, not in anger,
But in the way you once did,
Soft, warm, familiar.

But when I open them,
There is only silence,
And the echo of a love
That never left my bones.

Paper Thin.

They say time heals,
But my wounds are paper-thin,
One touch, one word,
And they tear open again.

I wrap myself in resilience,
Fold myself into origami strength,
But even the strongest paper
Can crumble in the rain.

Maybe one day,
I will be carved in stone,
Unbreakable.
But for now,
I remain paper-thin.

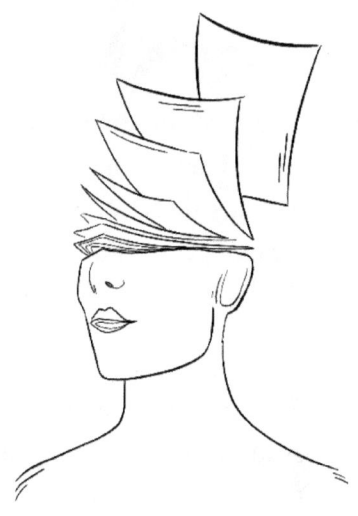

Unfinished Sentences.

You were my favorite story,
But we never made it to the last page.
The ink dried too soon,
Leaving me with half-written chapters
And questions without answers.

Do you still think of me?
Or did you close the book
And place it on a forgotten shelf,
Collecting dust like a past
That never truly mattered?

Hollow Home.

This house still holds your footprints,
Your scent lingers in the air,
The walls still whisper your name,
Yet you are nowhere.

I walk these halls like a stranger,
Haunted by a love that once made it
a home.
Now, it's just a hollow space,
Filled with echoes of laughter
That turned into silence.

Hands That No Longer Hold.

Once, my fingers fit between yours
Like puzzle pieces meant to be.
Now, they are just hands,
Empty, cold, foreign.

I reach out sometime's,
Only to remember,

There is nothing left to hold,
Nothing left to lose.

The Last Goodbye.

If I had known that was the last time,
I would have held on longer.
I would have memorized the way you breathed,
The way your lips curled before a laugh.

I would have whispered my love
Like a prayer against your skin,
One last time,
So maybe, just maybe,
It would echo in your soul
Long after you walked away.

Smoke And Silence.

Your words once set me on fire,
Now, I sit in the ashes.
Burnt-out,
Weightless,
Vanishing into the silence
Like smoke from a dying flame.

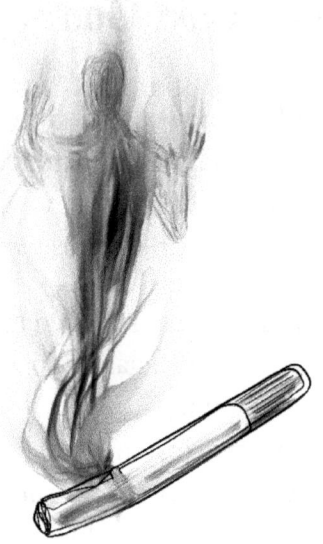

Weightless.

I once carried the world on my shoulders,
dragging chains of doubt and expectations,
walking roads paved by others,
wearing masks of who they wanted me to be.

But today, the air feels lighter,
the wind no longer fights me, it guides me.
My heart beats to its own rhythm,
my feet walk paths carved by my own hands.

I have let go.
Of the voices telling me who I should be.
Of the fears whispering that I am not enough.
Of the past that tried to keep me caged.

Now, I stand on the edge of endless possibility,
breathing in the scent of my own freedom.
No weight, no chains, no fear.
Only the sky, open and waiting.

Unshaken.

I have seen storms,
winds strong enough to bend even the mightiest trees.
I have walked through fire,
burned and broken, waiting to turn to ash.

But here I stand,
with breath still in my lungs,
with a heart that still knows how to love.

I count my blessings,
not in riches or things,
but in the way my mother still remembers my name,
the way my friends still laugh with me,
the way the sky still welcomes me every morning.

I have lost,
but I have gained so much more.
I have fallen,
but I have risen stronger.

If this is not a blessing,
then what is?

The Recipe for Laughter.

Take one terrible joke,
sprinkle in some sarcasm,
add a pinch of bad timing,
and watch laughter bubble over like a boiling pot.

Stir in a handful of old memories,
a teaspoon of embarrassing moments,
and a generous amount of someone
who knows your weird.

Now let it sit,
until it's the middle of the night,
when every word is suddenly ten
times funnier,
and laughter turns into a silent
struggle to breathe.

Laughter is messy,
it's contagious,
it's the kind of chaos we all secretly love.
And the best part?
It doesn't need a reason.

Golden Hour.

The world slows down at golden hour.
The sun lingers, stretching its arms,
painting the sky in shades of fire and
honey.

The wind hums a lullaby,
the waves kiss the shore one last
time before nightfall,
the earth exhales, soft and slow.

And for a moment,
just a single, fleeting moment,
everything feels… okay.

Not perfect.
Not extraordinary.
Just enough.

And maybe, that's all I ever needed.

Echoes of Us.

There are days when I swear I hear you in the wind,
your laughter carried in the hum of the trees,
your voice in the whispers of passing strangers.

There are nights when the silence echoes with your absence,
like a song that never reaches its final note.
But even as memories pull at my heart,
I do not break.

I sit with the echoes,
I let them drift around me,
until they are nothing more than fading ripples on the water.

I do not chase them.
I do not drown in them.
I simply let them pass.

Wild and Untamed.

I am not meant to be tamed,
not built for cages wrapped in golden chains.
I am the wind that refuses to be held,
the fire that does not ask permission to burn.

They called me reckless,
they called me too much,
too wild, too loud, too free,
but the sun does not apologize for shining,
and neither will I.

The Art of Letting Go.

They say letting go is like releasing a balloon,
watching it rise, further and further,
until it's nothing but a speck in the sky.

But no one talks about the aching fingers,
how tight you held on,
how much you fought the wind trying to steal it
away.

No one talks about the weight that lingers in your
palm,
the ghost of something once held so dear.

Letting go is an art,
one that I am still learning.

But today, my hands are open.
And that is enough.

Midnight Conversations with Myself.

I ask myself the same questions at 2 AM,
over and over like a broken record.

"Am I doing enough?"
"Will I ever be enough?"
"What if I never get where I want to be?"

But the stars do not rush the sunrise.
The ocean does not apologize for taking its time to reach the shore.
So why do I treat my growth like a race?

I am unfolding.
I am learning.
I am enough.
even in the in-between.

The Softest Kind of Love.

Love is not always loud,
not always fireworks and grand gestures.

Sometimes, love is quiet.
It is the steady presence of someone who stays,
the warmth of hands that do not let go.

It is a cup of tea on a tired evening,
a gentle voice saying, "I got you,"
a soft glance across a crowded room,
knowing you are safe where you stand.

Love does not always need words.
Sometimes,

it is simply…

there.

The Weight of Silence.

There are nights when silence feels heavier than words,
where the quiet fills the room like an unwelcome guest.

I scroll through conversations left unanswered,
stare at my reflection in dimly lit windows,
wondering if anyone
truly sees me.

I reach for the phone,
but stop myself.
Because the truth is,
if they wanted to talk to
me,
they would have.

So I sit with the silence,
let it settle in my bones.

And maybe, just maybe,
one day it won't feel so heavy anymore.

Moonlit Roads.

There's something about driving at night,
headlights carving a path through the unknown,
the hum of the engine in sync with the rhythm of my thoughts.

The road stretches ahead, endless and uncertain,
but for once, I am not afraid.

I do not need a map,
I do not need a destination.
I only need the courage to keep driving,
to chase the horizon until I find what I'm looking for.

Even if I don't know what that is just yet.

The Sound of Unfinished Goodbyes.

There are goodbyes wrapped in finality,
sealed with the weight of certainty.
And then there are the ones that linger,
half-spoken, unfinished,
like an unsent letter,
a call that was never made.

I wonder if you still think about it,
if the words we never said still echo between us.
Or maybe,
you've long since turned the page,
while I am still holding onto the last line.

Chasing Sunsets.

I used to chase happiness like it was something distant,
something waiting at the end of the road,
just beyond my grasp.

But then I realized,
happiness is not found in tomorrows,
not in "someday" or "when I finally…"
It is here, in this moment.

In the golden hues of a setting sun,
in the laughter shared over coffee,
in the way the wind dances through my hair.

Happiness was never ahead of me.
It was beside me all along.

The Beauty of Beginning Again.

There is beauty in the breaking,
in the moments when life shatters,
when everything we knew is torn apart.

Because in that breaking,
there is space,
space to rebuild,
space to grow,
space to start again.

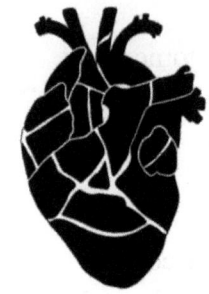

And maybe,
this time,
it will be even more beautiful than before.

Your Future Self Is Cheering for You.

Somewhere in the future,
there's a version of you who laughs easier,
loves louder,
and sleeps peacefully through the night.

They are so proud of you for fighting through the days you wanted to give up.
They're cheering for you,
even now,
especially now.

Coming Home.

Living abroad teaches you things no classroom
ever could.
You begin to notice how precious time really is,
how the little routines at home suddenly feel
like rare treasures,
how family dinners you once overlooked now
feel like sacred rituals.

You start cherishing the sound of familiar laughter,
the smell of home-cooked meals,
and the way your friends make everything feel just
like it used to,
even if life has changed.

Being away shifts your perspective.
You realize that success isn't always about chasing something new,
sometimes, it's about returning to what's always been there.
The warmth of family,
the comfort of old jokes,
the peace of being known without needing to explain yourself.

Vacations back home stop being breaks from life,
they become reminders of what really matters in it.

On the Edge of Sadness.

I'm not sad,
but I can feel the weight of it nearby,
like a storm resting just beyond the horizon.

I stand still,
feet planted firmly on the ground,
breathing through the ache I can't quite
name.

It's not darkness.
It's not light.
It's something in between,
a quiet place where I choose to stay,
holding my heart steady against the pull.

Ghost of You.

I walk through the streets we once roamed,
Every corner whispers your name,
But it's not you.
It's the shadow of your absence,
Lingering like a cigarette's last ember,
Fading, but never gone.
I reach for you in my dreams,
Only to wake up with clenched fists,
Holding nothing but the ghost of you.

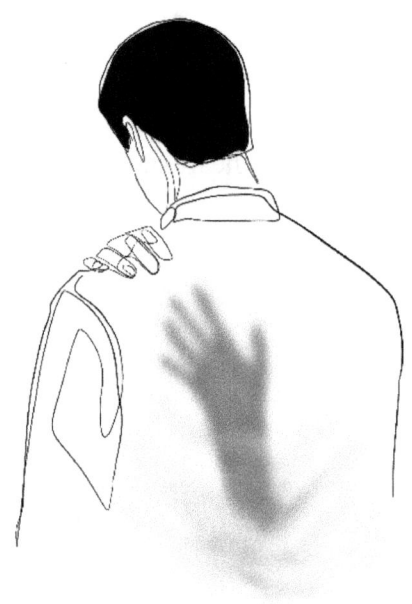

The Good Moments.

Some days, the world feels heavy.
But then,
a song you love plays in a café,
a friend sends you a meme so ridiculous you snort laugh,
the sky decides to be a painting just because it can.

Life never promised only sunshine.
But it *does* leave little gifts
everywhere,
waiting for you to notice.

Look closer.
There's still so much good here.

Reasons to Stay.

Stay for the mornings you haven't seen yet,
for the songs you haven't heard,
for the people you haven't laughed with.
Stay for the quiet victories,
the unexpected kindness,
the days that start heavy and end in laughter.
Stay,

because the good is still out there,
waiting to find you.

The Art of Not Taking Life Too Seriously.

Spill the coffee.
Laugh when you trip.
Text your best friend a meme at 2 a.m.
Wear the outfit that makes you feel like a work of art.
Life isn't an exam you have to pass.
It's a messy, beautiful thing you get to dance through.

The Kind of Happiness That Stays.

It's not always fireworks and grand moments.
Sometimes, happiness comes quietly,
in the smell of coffee filling a small kitchen,
in the warmth of sunlight hitting your skin on a
slow afternoon.
It's laughing without checking who's watching,
or finding a song that feels like it knows your heart
better than you do.

It's not loud. It's not flashy.
It's a kind of happiness that sits beside you,
asks nothing from you,
and says,

"You're allowed to enjoy this. You're allowed to be okay."

The best kind of joy doesn't demand attention,
it simply reminds you that life, even when messy,
still holds so much beauty.

Healing Looks Like This.

It's messy hair and cancelled plans.
It's deep breaths in crowded rooms.
It's laughing again without feeling guilty.
It's opening the curtains, even when you're tired.
Healing isn't loud.
Sometimes, it's just choosing to stay soft in a
world that tries to harden you.

For No Reason At All.

Laugh hard.
Laugh badly.
Laugh until your stomach hurts.
It doesn't need to be deep, or meaningful, or fixed to a reason.
Joy is allowed to be unreasonable.
In fact, it's better that way.

Little Victories.

Getting out of bed.
Making your bed.
Remembering to drink water.
Not spiraling over something that would've
wrecked you last year.
Little victories count too.
In fact, they build the strongest
kind of life.

Conversations With Myself.

Me: I'm a disaster.
Also me: A *charming* disaster.
Me: I have no idea what I'm doing.
Also me: Same. Let's keep going.

We're doing better than we think.

You Deserve Lightness Too.

Not every day has to be a battle.
You deserve days filled with laughter,
hours spent doing nothing important,
moments of forgetting the weight you carry.
You were never meant to suffer just because you
feel deeply.
Let yourself breathe.

The Heart of Home.

Family isn't just who you
share a name with,
it's who you share silence
with and still feel
understood.
It's the laughter echoing
from the kitchen,
the casual way someone
remembers how you like
your tea,
the safety in knowing you don't have to be perfect here.

They're the people who've seen every version of you,
the curious child, the stubborn teenager,
the dreamer who packed their bags and left to find themselves.
And through it all, they stayed.

With family, love doesn't always need to be spoken.
It's folded into laundry,
passed down in recipes,
and wrapped in warm embraces at the door.

No matter how far you go,
no matter how much life changes,
there's a piece of your heart that always lives with them.
Because family isn't just part of your story.
They are the place your story began.

Joy, Inconveniently.

Joy doesn't always show up on time.
It doesn't knock politely or wait until you're ready.
Sometimes it barges in during a bad hair day,
spills your coffee,
and makes you laugh in the middle of
crying.

It's awkward.

It's inconvenient.
But it saves you anyway.
Let it.

Bad Days Aren't Forever.

One bad day doesn't erase the good ones.
One heartbreak doesn't cancel out all love.
One storm doesn't mean the sun forgot you.
Bad days pass.
Good days come back.
Hold on,

you're closer than you think.

The friendship checklist.

Friendship is basically:

- Roasting each other lovingly
- Sending cursed memes
- Saying "I'm outside" 3 minutes after making plans
- Hyping each other up like unpaid therapists
- Knowing you're stuck with each other for life

And being grateful for it.

Joy is Rebellious.

Smiling anyway is an act of rebellion.
Loving anyway is an act of courage.
Choosing joy,

even when it's hard,
that's not weakness.
That's strength in its purest form.

I Bet You'd Ruin My Routine

I like my peace,
my soft mornings and slow evenings.
But something tells me
you'd make me stay up late,
laugh louder,
and suddenly crave coffee with two cups
instead of one.
I'd complain,
but secretly?
I think I'd love the chaos of you.

Joy Found Me Anyway.

I wasn't looking for it.
I was busy surviving,
busy keeping my head down,
busy pretending I didn't need
anything else.

And then, one day,
in the middle of all the chaos,
joy found me anyway.

It came in the way the light fell across the floor.
It came in the way a stranger held the door open.
It came in the way my favorite song played at the perfect moment.

Tiny things.
Insignificant things.
But they stitched something broken inside me back together.

Joy doesn't always wait for you to be ready.
Sometimes,

 it just shows up,
gentle and stubborn,
refusing to let you stay lost forever.

You're Allowed to Outgrow Things.

You're allowed to outgrow sadness.
You're allowed to outgrow fear.
You're allowed to outgrow the versions of you
that only knew survival.

You're allowed to grow into joy,
into boldness,
into a life so good it surprises even you.

Outgrowing pain isn't betrayal.
It's proof that you made it.

Simple Magic.

There's magic in slow mornings,
in the first sip of coffee,
in the way your favorite song can turn an entire day around.

There's magic in clean sheets,
open windows,
unexpected laughter.

We wait for the big miracles,
but forget that the small ones are everywhere.
Quiet. Unassuming.
Changing everything in their own gentle way.

Before It Ended

Before it fell apart,
before the silence,
before the sharp words and broken glances
we were something beautiful.

I won't pretend we weren't.
And I won't rewrite the past to ease the ache.
Because for a while,
we loved each other well.
And that deserves to be remembered,
even if it didn't last.

Your Life is Already a Story Worth Telling.

You don't have to climb mountains,
cross oceans,
or have a thousand victories to be proud of your life.

You woke up today.
You kept going when it would've been easier to stop.
You found small joys tucked between hard moments.
You cared,

you tried,

you loved,
even when it scared you.

That's enough.
That's more than enough.
Your story is already something beautiful.

It Will Be Good Again.

Not just better, good.

The kind of good that fills
your chest with peace.
The kind of good that feels
like soft laughter shared with
someone who understands.
The kind of good that wraps
around you quietly when you're
not even looking.

It won't always hurt this much.
One day,

you'll wake up and realize,
the heaviness left without saying goodbye,
and in its place,
lightness bloomed.

You Are Allowed to Shine.

You don't have to hide the bright parts of yourself.
You don't have to dim your laughter,
your dreams,
your joy.

The world needs people who smile for
no reason.
People who dream out loud.
People who live like they believe
beautiful things are still possible.

You are allowed to be one of them.
Shine, even when it feels easier to stay small.
You were made to be seen.
You were made to glow.

A Reminder: You're Doing Great.

You're doing better than you think.
You made it through awkward conversations,
through days when you wanted to throw your phone into a lake,
through mornings when the bed was holding you hostage.

You remembered to drink water.
You answered that one text you were avoiding.
You survived another meeting that could have been an email.

This is hero-level living.
Give yourself some credit.

Life Advice, From Me to You.

Eat the cake.

Dance even if you look ridiculous.

Wear the outfit you almost talked yourself out of.

Start the thing you're scared to start.

Laugh at your own jokes.

Cry if you need to,

 but don't unpack and live there.

You're not here to be perfect.
You're here to live.

There's No Rush.

You don't have to figure everything out by next Thursday.
You don't have to have a five-year plan color-coded and laminated.
You don't have to panic if you're still
Googling

"how to be an adult" at 2 a.m.

Life isn't a race.
It's a messy,
Beautiful,
hilarious journey.
You're allowed to stumble.
You're allowed to make weird turns.
You're allowed to enjoy it even when
it makes no sense.

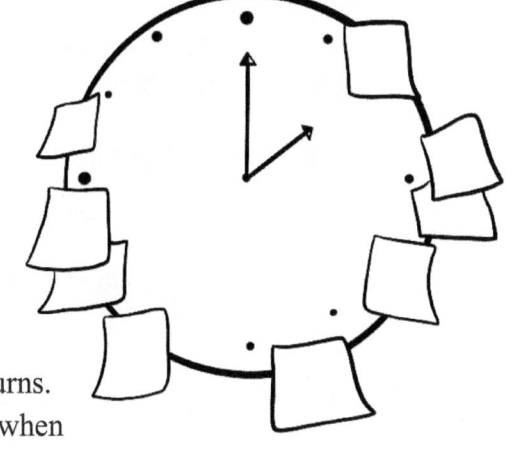

The Official Survival Kit.

Things you actually need to survive life.

A playlist that understands your soul.

Friends who send you memes instead of deep emotional advice.

Snacks hidden in at least three locations.

The ability to ugly-laugh at least once a week.

A tiny piece of hope you refuse to let go of, no matter what

Everything else is optional.

Some Days You're the Poem.

Some days you're a disaster.
Some days you're a masterpiece.
And some days, you're a weird little poem that makes no sense,
but somehow makes people smile anyway.

You're still worth reading.
Always.

You're Trouble, Aren't You?

The way you talk.
The way you look away when you smile.
You've got all the signs of being the
kind of person
my friends would warn me about.
But tell me again
how that makes it any less tempting?

You Don't Have to Make Sense.

You are allowed to be a mess and still be magic.
Allowed to be confused and still be courageous.
Allowed to change your mind,
start over on a Tuesday afternoon,
cry over a TV commercial,
and laugh about it five minutes later.

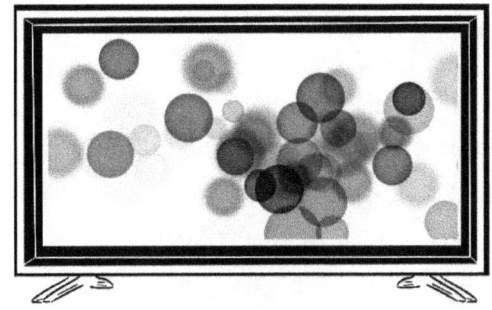

You don't have to make sense.
You just have to be real.

Laugh First, Question Later.

If you ever wonder whether you should
laugh at something,
the answer is probably yes.
Laugh first.
Question it later.

Life's serious enough.
You deserve to let joy sneak up on you,
even when it makes absolutely no sense.

The Small Wins Matter.

Did you make your bed? Victory.
Did you text back? Champion.
Did you drink water and not just caffeine today? Living legend.

Every small thing you do to take care of yourself is a rebellion against the idea that you have to be perfect to be proud.

Celebrate every single one.
You're doing better than you know.

You Are the Plot Twist.

Everyone loves a good story with an unexpected twist.
Guess what?
You're it.

You are the moment everything shifts.
The plot thickens.
The clouds clear.
The main character realizes they were
powerful all along.

You're not stuck.
You're building suspense.
And soon, you're going to shock
even yourself
with how far you go.

Self-Love, Softly

I used to wait for someone to love me like this
with gentleness, with patience,
with the kind of attention that says,
"I see you, even in your quiet."

But I grew tired of waiting.
So I became the one
who held myself at midnight,
who cooked dinner with music playing,
who stood in front of the mirror
and whispered,
"You are still worth everything."

And now?
I don't need to be chosen to feel full.
I already am.

The Universe Has a Sense of Humor.

You ever notice how life gives you exactly what you need, right after you stop obsessing over it?

You let go.
You sigh and say, *"Fine, whatever."*
And suddenly, *boom.*
There's the opportunity. The answer.
The moment.

Maybe the universe is just waiting for us to unclench.
Maybe it likes a good punchline too.

How to Be Happy (According to Me).

Step one: Lower the bar.
If you laughed today, you win.
If you found a good snack, you win.
If you survived another round of *existential dread*, congratulations,

you win again.

Step two: Stop trying to impress people who wouldn't notice if you turned into a literal beam of sunlight.

Step three: Dance. Even badly. Especially badly.

Happiness isn't complicated.
It's built out of tiny, ridiculous moments strung together like fairy lights.

You're Allowed to Be a Little Ridiculous.

Take selfies that look more like cryptid sightings.
Sing off-key at red lights.
Make dumb jokes no one but you finds funny.

This is your life,
not a movie you need to edit for the critics.

Be ridiculous.
Be loud about what you love.
Be wildly, gloriously human.

The world is already too serious.
You don't have to be.

Someday You'll Be Glad You Didn't Quit.

There's a version of you in the future,
wearing a ridiculously comfortable hoodie,
drinking something warm,
smiling at a sunset you almost didn't get to see.

And they're thinking,
"Thank you for not giving up. Thank you for fighting through the days that felt impossible."

They're living a life you're building right now,
one stubborn, brave step at a time.

The Good You Cannot See.

Somewhere right now,
someone is laughing so hard they can't catch their breath.
Somewhere, a heart is healing without even realizing it.
Somewhere, the sky is opening into a sunset so
beautiful it'll make a stranger stop in
awe.

Good things are happening.
even if you can't see them yet.
Even if you're not there to witness
them.

One day, that good will find its way
to you.
Like sunlight slipping quietly through a window,
like joy waiting patiently at your doorstep.

Congratulations: You're Weird.

You care too much.
You laugh too loud.
You dream too big.
You feel too deeply.

Congratulations.
You're officially weird.
The good kind. The kind that makes the world a little less dull.
The kind that makes life a little more real.

Please don't ever stop.
The world needs more of your kind of magic.

Today is a Good Day to Begin, Again.

Maybe yesterday was heavy.
Maybe last week was confusing.
Maybe the last few years have been something you still don't have words for.

But today,
today is a blank page.

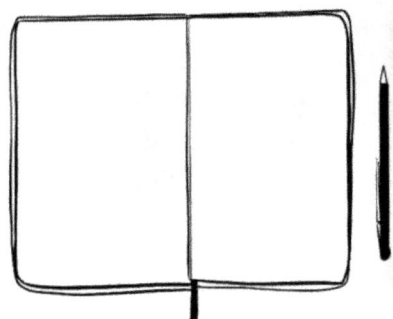

No one's asking you to get it all right.
Just pick up the pen.
Try again.
Begin again.
As many times as you need to.
You are allowed infinite chances to choose yourself.

You Make Me Forget My Standards

I have rules.
Boundaries.
A very clear list of red flags.
But then you smiled,
and suddenly I'm rewriting everything
because apparently,
"they're cute though"
counts as a valid exception now.

Eyes That Talk Too Much

You didn't say a word.
But your eyes?
They wrote entire paragraphs
about maybe, about wanting,
about what we'd never dare admit out loud.
And I read every single one.

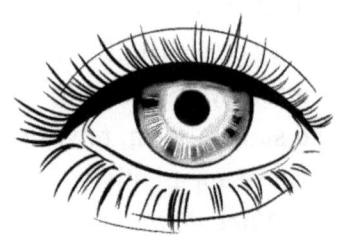

Safe Love

Love, to me, isn't loud.
It doesn't shout to be seen
or demand to be chased.

It's a hand reaching for yours in the dark.
A steady voice when you doubt your worth.
It's choosing each other on the quiet days,
not just the beautiful ones.

Love, real love, is peace.
And when it comes,
you won't feel uncertain
you'll feel safe.

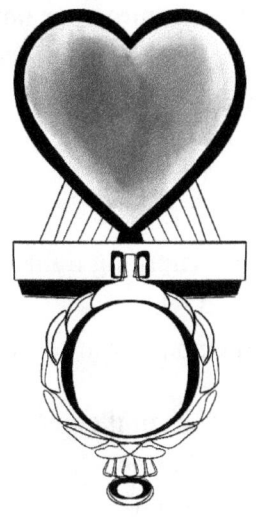

When Love is Easy

There's a kind of love that doesn't make you question yourself.
Doesn't turn your heart into a battlefield.
Doesn't leave you wondering if you're too
much,
or not enough.

It just fits.
Like morning light through the
window,
like music you forgot you loved.

And when it comes
you'll know.
Because peace feels
different
when you've spent years
calling chaos love.

The Love That Waits Quietly

Maybe love isn't late.
Maybe it's just waiting for me to arrive
not at a place,
but at a version of myself
that no longer begs to be chosen.
The kind of self that stands whole,
so when love does come,
it's not a rescue,
but a recognition.

Just So You Know

I noticed you.
Not just your face
but how you tilt your head
when you laugh,
how you speak like your
words matter,
how you make ordinary look
interesting.
I noticed.
And if you're lucky,
I might let you notice me back.

Midnight Thoughts About Someone I Haven't Met

I wonder if they sleep peacefully.
If their laugh comes easily,
if they hum when they cook,
if they know someone out there
already cares for the shape of their heart
without even knowing their name.
It's strange
how we can miss someone
who's still a stranger.

Not a Fairytale

I don't need a perfect love.
Not the kind they write songs about,
not the sweeping grand gestures.

Give me the simple things
A kiss on the forehead.
A shared silence that feels like home.
Someone who stays.

That's my fairytale now
real, quiet, unwavering.

Loving Life, Slowly

I'm falling in love again
not with a person,
but with how the sky changes colors,
how laughter finds me in unlikely places,
how peace has a sound
when the world finally quiets.

This kind of love doesn't need to be held
only noticed.

If You Ever Arrive

If you ever find me
find me whole.
Not in the ruins of my past,
not in the echoes of who I used to be.

Find me blooming.
Soft, sure, and unapologetically alive.
I don't want to be rescued.
I want to be met.
And if we love
let it be as equals,
not saviors.

Soft Crush

It's not serious.
Just a soft kind of liking.
The kind that makes your name feel warm in
my mouth.
The kind that turns 'maybe'
into
*"I hope they're thinking about me
too."*

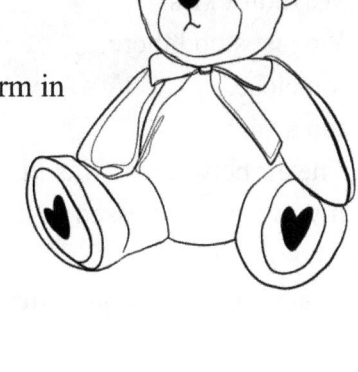

Almost

We didn't kiss.
We just stood there,
too close,
too aware.
The air between us wasn't silence
it was tension dressed as patience.
And honestly?
That almost was louder than any touch.

Call Me Dramatic

But the way your name shows up on my screen?
It's cinematic.
Like background music starts playing
and I forget whatever I was doing
because suddenly
you're the only plot that matters.

The Story I Now Write

There was a time when I thought love was the answer to everything, when I believed that giving my all meant I would receive the same in return. But I have learned that not all love is meant to last, and not every goodbye is a loss.

I have been broken, but I have healed.
I have been lost, but I have found myself.
I have been silenced, but now, I speak with conviction.

You can lose yourself in love, but you can also find yourself in its absence.
And maybe, just maybe, the greatest love story is the one you write for yourself.

This is no longer a story of heartbreak.
This is a story of survival, of healing, of rebirth.
The ink has dried on the past, and now, I turn the page.

A new chapter begins.

www.ingramcontent.com/pod-product-compliance
Lightning Source LLC
Chambersburg PA
CBHW050525170426
43201CB00013B/2084